YELLOWSTONE
AND THE
FIRES OF CHANGE

George Wuerthner

1988

HAGGIS HOUSE PUBLICATIONS, INC.

A bison herd wades a river. Photo by Erwin and Peggy Bauer.

Published by Haggis House Publications, Inc. P.O. Box
    26905, Salt Lake City, Utah 84126-0905
Distributed exclusively by Dream Garden Press P.O. Box
    27076, Salt Lake City, Utah 84127

Photographs copyright © by the respective photographers.
Front cover photograph: Flaming forest, by Jim Peaco,
    courtesy National Park Service.
Title page photograph: Smoke-obscured sun, by Paul
    Fraughton.
Back cover photograph: Clover-Mist Fire, by Jim Peaco,
    courtesy National Park Service.

Design by Richard Firmage
FIRST EDITION — 1988
10 9 8 7 6 5 4 3 2 1
ISBN: 0-942688-70-8

For complete ordering information write or call:
DREAM GARDEN PRESS
P.O. BOX 27076
SALT LAKE CITY, UTAH 84127
1-800-322-5758

Write for free catalog.

ACKNOWLEDGEMENTS

I would like to thank the many researchers and scientists whose published papers, articles and books contributed substantially to my understanding of fire ecology and the Yellowstone ecosystem. In addition, a number of Yellowstone National Park employees were especially helpful in the research and preparation of this book. They include: Chief Park Naturalist George Robinson; Public Affairs Spokeswoman, Amy Vanderbilt; Park Biologist, Don Despain; Park Historian, Tim Manns; and Park Photo Specialist, Jim Peaco. My wife, Mollie Matteson, edited the entire manuscript and contributed significantly to its improved readability. Thanks should also go to those who shaped the manuscript into a book: Bob Petersen, Ken Sanders, Richard Firmage and the people involved in the printing and typesetting.

CONTENTS

Flames climb up through a forest along the Firehole River. Photo by George Wuerthner.

INTRODUCTION

T HE summer of 1988 will go down in history as one of the driest ever recorded in the Rocky Mountains and northern Great Plains. Crops shriveled in fields, rivers shrank to trickles, while forests and meadows baked under a

cloudless sky for weeks on end. The drought of 1988 exceeded the records set during the Dust Bowl years of the 1930s. Despite the unmatched weather statistics of the summer, however, to many people the most conspicuous result of the 1988 drought was the swarm of wildfires that burned throughout the West—in particular those which charred the lands in and around Yellowstone National Park. Nurtured by hot, dry weather, drought, abundant fuel and winds gusting to 80 mph, more than fifty wildfires crept, and sometimes raced, across nearly 1.38 million acres in the Greater Yellowstone area. These fires, the largest and most extensive in the park's 116 year history, riveted the attention of the nation on its first national park and stunned the world with their display of nature's sometimes unstoppable power.

Daily television, radio and press coverage brought vivid details of these historic blazes into every home, and news of the fire fighting efforts were watched as intently as were the reports on our forces in the Vietnam War two decades earlier. Indeed, a virtual army of firefighters—ten thousand of them—converged on the park along with 229 pumper trucks and 57 helicopters. By early autumn, the military itself was brought into the fray: the Army deployed 2,336 soldiers from Fort Lewis, Washington; the

These fires, the largest and most extensive in the park's 116 year history, riveted the attention of the nation on its first national park and stunned the world with their display of nature's sometimes unstoppable power.

Marines sent two battalions from Camp Pendleton, California. The soldiers were welcome relief for the exhausted civilian crews. Before the fires were quenched more than a 120 million dollars had been spent, but given their magnitude the fires caused a surprisingly small amount of damage to property and life. One firefighter, Edward Hutton, was killed on October 11th by a falling charred tree while he was doing mop-up work on the Shoshone National Forest along the eastern perimeter of the Clover-Mist fire. Property damage was confined to less than twenty structures—mostly isolated cabins—that were burned.

Despite the potential danger of these large fires, and the immensity of the firefighting effort, the National Park Service was able to keep at least some parts of the park open all but one day (September 10th) of the entire fire season. This gave millions of tourists an unparalleled opportunity to see first-hand how wildfires burn and what impacts they have on the landscape. However, similar to the experience of those who may witness a volcanic eruption, the "spectacle" is more often than not rather uninspiring. Active volcanoes usually fume and sputter, with perhaps only a rare explosion. Likewise, wildfires most often creep along the ground, producing more smoke than flame. Fire "blow ups" are relatively infrequent, but, as with a violent volcanic eruption, a roaring, speeding fire

Firefighters putting out small blazes. Photo by Jim Peaco/NPS.

front is among the most frightening and awesome of all natural phenomena.

In the minds of many people, the fires destroyed Yellowstone. Acrimonious editorials and letters in newspapers across the country criticized the Park Service's management policies and suggested that the widespread fires could have been avoided or at least controlled if the agency had only dealt with them swiftly. Common to many of the critics was their idea that fires can be switched on or off like a light switch. They accused the Park Service of not shutting the fires down when it appeared that Yellowstone would be reduced to ashes. Their indignant voices sounded all the way to Washington, D.C. with help from the congressional delegations of the states surrounding the park, who joined in denouncing the Park Service and promised congressional investigations into its fire management polices.

However, there were others—fire specialists, ecologists, naturalists and some people who have either studied fire behavior or fought fires under severe conditions such as existed in Yellowstone that summer—who felt that there was little that could have been done to stop the wildfires. Also, even if outright suppression had been possible, it is likely most of these people would have opposed such

When people visit Yellowstone and gaze out upon the landscape with an appreciative eye, they are seeing a fire-created environment.

action. From an ecologist's perspective, it is the suppression of fires, not the fires themselves, which is truly destructive. Wildfires are the dominant driving force behind the Yellowstone ecosystem, just as rain is to the tropical rainforests. Yellowstone forests and grasslands have evolved under an environmental regime of periodic fire, and are now as dependent upon fire as the tropical rainforests are dependent upon rain to maintain the ecological character and makeup of the ecosystem.

When people visit Yellowstone and gaze out upon the landscape with an appreciative eye, they are seeing a fire-created environment. And because of the dynamic nature of a living landscape, we cannot preserve it in the same manner as we might preserve a building, rather, preservation requires change. But change must be within the parameters which have shaped the Yellowstone landscape for thousands of years. Wildfires cannot destroy Yellowstone; misguided attempts to suppress all fires can.

There is beauty even in a fire charred and smoking landscape as this scene by West Thumb shows. Photo by George Wuerthner.

HISTORIC SETTING

WILDFIRES started by lightning have always been a major evolutionary influence upon the western landscape. Even fossilized chunks of charcoal (called "fusain") and fossilized fire scars have been found among the petrified forests in

Yellowstone; and they provide ample evidence that wild-fires have been a part of the Yellowstone region for millions of years!

Scientists have discovered that they can reconstruct the fire history of an area by examining fire scar tissue on tree ring samples of trees that were burned, but not killed in past fires. By correlating the occurrence of these fire scars, they can determine within a year or two when a major fire occurred. These studies have shown that in some ecosystems, such as the drier, low-elevation pon-derosa pine forests throughout the West, fires may have occurred as frequently as as every three to five years. Such fires were usually relatively "cool" and consumed little more than the dead tops of grasses leaving the roots intact from which the plant sprouted new shoots the following spring. The thick-barked boles of the ancient mature pines were unharmed and the resulting forests were often described by early travelers as being "open and park-like," with the old pines somewhat evenly spaced like the pillars of a Greek temple.

. . . fossilized fire scars found among the petrified forests in Yellowstone, which provide ample evidence that wildfires have been a part of the Yellowstone region for millions of years!

Conversely, higher and wetter environments such as the sub-alpine forests of Yellowstone or the old growth rainforests of the Pacific Northwest also burned on occa-sion, but the intervals were much longer—perhaps as long as every three hundred to four hundred years or more. Though fires were uncommon, the greater accumulations of fuel meant that when they occurred the fires were often catastrophic, stand-destroying conflagrations.

Most natural fires are started by lightning. One study found that between 1940 and 1975 there were 79,131 lightning-caused wildfires in the Rockies alone! And between 1972 and 1987 Yellowstone drew at least 369 lightning strikes that ignited fires in the park. Most of these fires went out after burning less than an acre. Of the 35,978 acres which did burn during this period, more than 95 percent of the acreage charred can be attributed to just a handful of fires.

Historically, lightning was not the only fire-starting agent. There are well-documented reports of fires set by Indians and frontiersmen, who used fire to clear out brush, drive enemies from hiding, or to stimulate new plant growth to attract wildlife. The journals of many early travelers and explorers make numerous references to Indian-caused fires. Osborn Russell, a fur trapper who traveled extensively in the Yellowstone region, described how a war party of Blackfeet Indians set fire to nearby vegetation to drive his party from hiding while they were traveling along the Madison River in Yellowstone in 1835. And Lewis and Clark, who were the first to explore the headwaters of the Missouri and Columbia Rivers during their epic 1804-06 cross-continent journey, repeatedly made references to the Plains Indians' practice of setting fire to the prairie. With fire they signalled to other groups of Indians or cleared away dead, dry grass so that the succulent, new growth of the spring would attract grazing animals like bison closer to their villages.

Though Indians occasionally passed through Yellow-stone, and one small group called the Sheepeaters lived there year-round, it is uncertain how many fires they may have caused in the Yellowstone ecosystem. Because of their overall low numbers and the infrequency with which they passed through the area, the Indian influence on fires is likely to have been less than it was in other places, such as the Great Plains, for example.

Most natural fires are started by lightning. One study found that between 1940 and 1975 there were 79,131 lightning caused wildfires in the Rockies alone!

The fire scars of the region bear testimony to a number of large fires in the years prior to and just after the creation of Yellowstone Park in 1872. George Gruell, a fire researcher who has done studies on the fire history of the Teton and Yellowstone areas, suggests that major fires occurred in the region in 1765, 1840, 1865, and repeatedly between 1878 and 1885. He concludes that the physical makeup of nearly all the plant communities found in the region are the result of repeated fires.

Petrified trees on Specimen Ridge record the occurrence of past fires as fossil fire scars. Photo by Larry Ulrich.

An 1897 photo of Bunsen Peak just south of Mammoth shows the dead snags and young re-growth after a recent fire. Prior to fire suppression which began in Yellowstone in 1886, such sites were far more common than in recent years. Photo courtesy of National Park Service (NPS).

Nearly a hundred years later, fires again burned Bunsen Peak as this photo taken at approximately the same location shows. Notice the increase of conifers which had occurred at the base of the mountain since the previous picture. Photo by George Wuerthner.

When the Washburn-Langford-Doane Expedition explored Yellowstone in 1870, they found widespread smoke which they believed resulted from fires set by Indians. William Henry Jackson, one of America's first landscape photographers, complained about the "smoky haze that filled the air" while he was in the Tetons during the summer of 1878. And the following year, in 1879, the famous painter of Yellowstone and the Tetons, Thomas Moran (for whom Mount Moran in Grand Teton National Park is named) found it nearly impossible to sketch the Tetons because the smoke from forest fires obscured the mountains. In 1883, the builder of the National Hotel at Mammoth, Rufus Hatch, commenting about a tour of the Norris Geyser Basin said that it was "especially eerie, fires having decimated the woods, leaving many a gaunt stump that took on ominous contours in the night shadows."

When the Army was detailed to patrol and protect Yellowstone Park in 1886, they found a fire burning on Bunsen Peak just south of Mammoth. In his annual report on the park, acting Superintendent Captain Moses Harris wrote that "destructive forest fires have been raging in the Park during the greater portion of the present season. . . . the most destructive one, which was burning when I arrived in the Park, originated on the 14th of August last, near the East Fork of the Gardiner River, in full view from the Mammoth Hot Springs Hotel and about seven miles distant. This fire is still burning, and has extended over a tract of country some ten or twelve miles in length by three to five in width." The army attempted to suppress this blaze—with little success—making the first attempt at fire suppression ever undertaken by the federal government.

In 1897 T.S. Brandegee of the U.S. Geological Survey filed a report on the forests south of Yellowstone Park. He commented: "It is only occasionally that tracts of timber of merchantable size are found. . . . This condition

Smoke from the fires of 1988 along the Madison River similar to what early explorers encountered in the Greater Yellowstone area during the 1800s when uncontrolled wildfires often obsured the sky. Photo by George Wuerthner.

appears to be due simply and solely to fires which have swept over the country so completely and persistently that scarcely any part has been entirely exempt from them, while nearly all portions have been burned again and again within a generation."

The year 1919 featured one of the driest summers encountered since the park's establishment. Patrols put out 306 small fires; lightning started the biggest fire which burned 2,500 acres on Grizzly Peak. Altogether fires burned 6,388 acres that year and cost $30,000 to suppress. The summer of 1931 was another dry one. A fire started at Heart Lake on July 17th. By the second day it had traveled 5 1/2 miles and had grown to 8,000 acres. More than 600 men were brought in to battle the blaze, which jumped across part of Heart Lake and was spotting (that is, creating spot fires) more than a half mile ahead of the main fire front. Rain on July 29th, just 12 days after the fires began, quenched the flames. Total fire fighting costs were $87,000—an unheard-of amount of money back then. Total acreage burned within the park was 20,364.

In 1940, some 20,700 acres burned in what turned out to be the worst year for fire after 1931, that is, until the summer of 1988. More than a thousand men battled the flames until once again rain snuffed out the flames. The 1950s and 1960s were relatively quiet years with few fires of any consequence. Not until 1979, when 10,000 acres burned, and 1981 when 20,000 acres were scorched, did any significant burning occur within the park.

Yet despite this long history of fires in the park, the blazes of 1988 were the largest fires in more than a century. Several large fire complexes, not a single conflagration, were responsible for the vast acreage burned in 1988. The largest fires which burned in and around Yellowstone in 1988 include: the 390,590 acre Clover-Mist Fire; 400,100 acre North Fork Fire; 225,500 Huck-Mink Fire complex; 224,000 acre Snake River Fire complex; 107,847 acre Storm Creek Fire; 107,450 acre Wolf Lake Fire; 23,325 acre Fan Fire; and the 81,900 acre Hellroaring Fire. (Note:

Due to the spotty nature in which fires burn, less than half of this total acreage actually was charred, so acreage figures can be somewhat misleading.)

Yet, despite this long history of fires in the park, the blazes of 1988 were the largest fires in more than a century.

Five of the eight largest fires began outside of the park and yet accounted for more than half of the acreage burned inside Yellowstone. The Storm Creek fire which threatened Cooke City and Silver Gate began within National Forest wilderness to the north of the park. The actual flames which nearly engulfed these two communities were the result of "back fires" purposely set by firefighters. The object of a back fire is to reduce fuels in front of an advancing wildfire front so that it runs itself out, but in the instance of Cooke City the winds suddenly reversed, blowing the back fire towards the firefighters and the town.

Eight of the 1988 fires were started by human carelessness, not lightning. The massive North Fork Fire which threatened the Old Faithful Inn, West Yellowstone,

Smoke from the Clover Fire sends a smoke column high into the sky above the upper Lamar Valley. Photo by Sandy Nykerk.

Mammoth and Roosevelt Lodge was started by a wood-cutter outside of the park on the Targhee National Forest. Although firefighters were put on the blaze immediately, strong winds the next day drove the fire beyond the fire-lines and into the history books.

As large as the cumulative size of all these fires was, they are not unusual if viewed within a historic context. Periodically throughout the United States there have been "fire years" when vast acreages burned. Every one of these "fire years" was also characterized by severe drought. Among the larger historic fires are the Miramichi fire in 1825 which burned more than five million acres in New Brunswick and Maine; the Michigan fires in 1881 which charred more than two and a half million acres, and the 1910 fires which charred more than five million acres across the West, particularly in western Montana and Idaho. The 1910 fires were particularly devastating, burning more than three million acres in forty-eight hours, incinerating portions of several towns, and killing 85 people! Tree ring examinations by fire ecologist Bill Romme indicate that extensive, episodic fires occurred in Yellowstone in the early 1700s and around 1850.

Five of the eight largest fires began outside of the park and yet accounted for more than half of the acreage burned inside Yellowstone.

These big fires invariably developed after several small fires grew together to advance along a common front. Several of the larger fires of this summer also exhibited this behavior. For example, the 390,590 acre Clover-Mist fire began on July 9 as the Mist fire. The Clover fire was noted on July 11. The two fires had burned into one united front by July 22. Other fires including the Lovely, Fern and Shallow fires eventually joined the blaze to make up the Clover-Mist fire complex.

Though some of these fires of 1988 were initially allowed to burn unhindered, as the summer drought progressed with no appreciable precipitation in June and early July, the Yellowstone Park administration made the decision on July 15th to begin suppressing all new fires and began containment action on those which were already burning. As noted earlier, federal fire suppression activities began in Yellowstone National Park with the Army in 1886. Eventually, federal land management agencies including the Forest Service, Park Service, and Bureau of Land Management (BLM) made fire suppression one of their major missions. New fire suppression equipment and technology (including use of helicopters and airplanes), earlier detection, plus a greater understanding of fire behavior all combined to make fire suppression feasible over a large portion of the West.

At the same time that suppression became more effective, the campaign initiated early in this century to stop careless, human-caused fires began to show measurable success, especially after Smokey the Bear was introduced as the symbol of the program in 1945. As a result

of this effort, most of us were indoctrinated with the idea that all fires were automatically destructive and "bad". This attitude permeates even the way we describe fires. Most newspapers and T.V. reports emphasized how the Yellowstone fires "destroyed" so many acres. Writers reported on the "devastation" or the timber "wasted." Few commented about the new wildlife habitat "created" or the "healthier" forests, which inevitably result from wild-fires. Even after reports indicated that the park fires had less impact than was at first imagined, there was still talk that "recovery" and "rehabilitation" were necessary—words that imply that there was damage and destruction.

As large as the cumulative size of all these fires was, they are not unusual if viewed within a historic context.

Negative attitudes towards fire may also be traced to our collective religious heritage, in which Hell is an "inferno," and "fire and brimstone" is used to frighten sinners onto a more moral path, while those who do not heed the Word are consigned to "burn" forever. Hostile

A Douglas fir becomes a fiery torch as the North Fork Fire races through the northern part of the park near Mammoth. Photo by Jim Peaco/NPS.

landscapes throughout the West are littered with names such as "Devil's Kitchen," "Hell's Half Acre," Devil's Golfcourse," or "Firehole." Our language is biased against any positive or even value-neutral descriptions of wildfire, and it is thus not surprising that the perception that wildfires can be "good" is slow in coming. Likewise, the idea that fire suppression can be "destructive" is a long way from being widely accepted.

. . . most of us were indoctrinated with the idea that all fires were automatically destructive and "bad." This attitude permeates even the way we describe fires.

Nevertheless, these heretical ideas gained momentum among scientists and fire specialists during the 1960s and 1970s as fire research demonstrated that many ecosystems are not only adapted to fire, but dependent on them. This research did not necessarily lessen the importance of preventing fires caused by human carelessness, nor did it unquestionably support all fires as a benign natural force, but it did raise the question of whether fire suppression of all blazes was desirable. One measurable and—to most land managers—unfortunate result of the increasing effectiveness of fire suppression has been an abnormally high accumulation of fuels. And when these fuels are ignited (lightning is one natural phenonmenon we have not yet learned to control) the resulting fires are of course more difficult to put out.

Because immediate and full fire suppression is the general rule on most lands throughout the West, a dangerously high level of fuel continues to accumulate. Some scientists have suggested that if this fuel is not reduced, the likelihood of a major conflagration, on the scale of the 1910 burns or greater, is possible. Suppression, in effect, is building a time bomb, which if not dismantled by widespread natural and prescribed burns will ultimately bring on holocausts of a magnitude that will make the Yellowstone fires of 1988 seem small by comparison.

Research throughout the country has discovered and revealed the influence and effect that fires—both human and naturally ignited—have had in many ecosystems. The open Sequoia forests of the Sierra Nevada in California, the sawgrass prairies of the Everglades, the Fan Palm oases in the Mohave Desert and the "balds" found on high peaks in the Appalachian Mountains are a just a few examples of fire-maintained or fire-created natural environments. Many scientists feel that fires started by Indians were one of the chief reasons why trees were unable to invade the prairies in now well-forested states such as Wisconsin, Indiana, and Ohio. Once regular burning was stopped, the forest quickly reclaimed these areas.

Early photographs of Yellowstone also substantiate the claims that many areas of the Park were maintained by fire so as to appear more open and with less timber than we find today. Many of these photos also show fire-blackened areas as well as young, recently regenerated forests—presumably grown up after a forest fire.

As research findings were analysed, scientists began to understand when and where fires were likely to occur. For example, studies have shown that if the weather is cool, wet, and windless with high humidity and limited fuel, any ignition is unlikely to burn more than a few acres before it goes out—with or without assistance from human firefighters. Out of 233 fires between 1972 and 1987 which started within designated "natural areas" of the park (where lightning fires are allowed to burn without suppression), 205 went out before they had burned even an acre of land. Of the remaining fires, the largest burned only 7,396 acres, less than one-third of one percent of the park's total acreage. Even during the exceptionally dry summer of 1988, 48 of the 52 fires ignited by lightning burned less than an acre and went out by themselves. Thus, in a typical year, most fires remain small and seldom burn more than a few acres. Of the few fires which do burn a significant acreage, researchers found that these were important to nutrient cycling, reduction of fuel and thus fire hazard, and creation of habitat diversity.

It was because of such findings that the National Park Service and other federal agencies such as the U.S. Forest Service began to implement what became known as "let burn" policies. Let burn policies occur primarily in national parks and within federally designated wilderness areas where logging and other commercial extractive uses are prohibited. All other areas including commerically valuable timberlands and developed sites continued to be protected from fire.

Suppression, in effect, is building a time bomb, which if not dismantled by widespread natural and prescribed burns, will ultimately bring on holocausts of a magnitude that will make the Yellowstone fires of 1988 pale by comparison.

Though called a let burn policy, no federal agency simply allowed all fires to burn at will over the landscape. Before any fires were permitted to burn unsuppressed, each agency developed a fire management plan for each specific park or wilderness. Each plan laid out in precise terms under what conditions fires would be tolerated and allowed to burn unhindered as well as under what conditions fires would continue to be suppressed. After years of research which defined fuel accumulation, fire patterns, and ecological and climatic parameters within the park, a fire plan was developed in 1972 which designated two let burn areas. The area covered by this policy was substantially enlarged in 1975 to include most of the undeveloped portions of the park.

The fire management plan did not allow all fires to burn unhindered as many presume. More properly, it should be termed a "natural burn" policy since there were specific instances recognized within the plan when some fires would be attacked and suppressed even within the

Obsidian Creek and the Gallatin Range one month before the area burned in 1988. The landscape visitors gaze upon with an apprecia-tive eye is one created and maintained by fire. Photo by George Wuerthner.

boundaries of a designated let burn area. These exceptions include suppression of all fires caused by humans; any fires which threaten property or life; any fires which might cross park boundaries into other lands not covered by a let burn philosophy (many of the surrounding national forest lands outside of the park also have a let burn management prescription); and any fires which the park superintendent deemed should be put out for whatever reasons. Out of 369 lightning-caused fires between 1972 and 1987, 136 of them were suppressed for one of the above reasons. As mentioned, of the 233 which were allowed to burn without attack and suppression, 205 burned themselves out after covering an acre or less.

Because of statistics like those listed above, the let burn policy, as a rule, is far more cost-effective than immediate suppression—provided that fire suppression is not required later should blazes expand beyond prescription or in some way threaten life or property. Obviously, in 1988 this was the case. Suppression costs that year exceeded an estimated $120 million: this included suppression of eight human-caused fires, immediate suppression of twelve natural fires, and the containment of ten natural fires which originally had been allowed to burn, but which were later attacked.

While no long-term fire-fighting costs are available for Yellowstone, a sense of the monetary savings can be gleaned from recent figures on suppression and monitoring costs within let burn areas in U.S. Forest Service wilderness areas in the northern Rockies region. In 1987 there were eighty-seven fires within Forest Service let burn areas covered by fire plans. Eighty-four burned out on their own without suppression, with a total monitoring cost of $20,150. Three of the eighty-seven fires burned beyond the boundaries of prescribed areas and had to be suppressed. These three fires cost $77,000 to control—by normal standards these were relatively inexpensive fires to suppress. It is not unusual for fires of only one or two thousand acres to carry a suppression price tag of a million dollars or more. For this reason, had all 369 Yellowstone Park fires been suppressed since the first let burn fire plan was adopted in 1972, the cumulative cost of annually suppressing these fires could have been substantial.

FIRE STORM SEQUENCE
This sequence of six photos shows a fire driven by high winds approaching a Park Service cabin on the Blacktail Plateau. The vegetation is primarily sagebrush with grass, which provided an explosive fuel when fanned by winds. According to the NPS photographer who recorded this sequence, the rapid advance of the fire

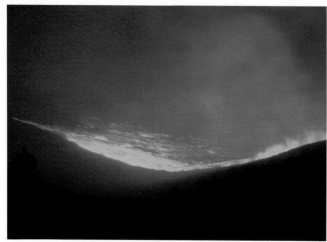

was frightening. While he photographed this scene he kept his car door open and the engine running. Flames exploded as if shot from a cannon, and were swept in front of the main fire as much as fifty feet or more. Trying to stop such a fire is impossible. Only when the winds died down did this rapid advance of the fires halt. All Photos by Jim Peaco/NPS.

A fire rages through the crown of the forest. Such roaring fires only occur under conditions of severe drought and high winds—conditions which dominated the summer of 1988. Photo by Jim Peaco/NPS.

THE CONDITIONS OF 1988

THE 1988 fire season officially started in Yellowstone National Park on May 24th when lightning struck a tree in the Lamar Valley. The tree burst into flames, but the fire went out—as had many others in years before—when rain quenched the burn several hours later. Another lightning bolt on June 23 ignited a blaze near Shoshone Lake in a remote part of the park's backcountry, but this fire did not go out. A month later, it forced the evacuation of Grant Village. The historic 1988 fire season was on.

What, if anything, went wrong? Was the Park Service responsible for ignoring all reason as some outspoken critics say? Could these massive fires have been suppressed, as many presume? The scientific research to date suggests a "no" answer to both of these questions. Given

Cottonwood trees in the Lamar Valley where lightning caused the first fire of the 1988 fire season. The blaze, like those created by most lightning strikes, went out on its own without any human suppression. Photo by George Wuerthner.

the conditions which prevailed during the summer of 1988, the conclusion of most fire specialists is that the large wildfires were unavoidable.

The convergence of several important factors made 1988 unique in recorded history. The preeminent agent of the extreme fire conditions was severe drought. Though summer drought is "normal" throughout much of the West including Yellowstone, the summer of 1988 was the driest ever recorded in the 116-year history of the park.

Secondly, in a "typical" summer, late June and July may be without rain, but August storms usually bring some rainfall to the region, dampening or extinguishing most fires which may have started earlier. This never happened in 1988. August remained dry and it was not until September 11th that any measurable precipitation was recorded.

The third factor was the unprecedented low moisture content of downed branches, grasses and timber. Frequently greater than 16 percent in most years, their moisture content was as low as two or three percent (kiln-dried lumber is twelve percent). The fuels also dried out much earlier that summer, and stayed dry much later than in a typical year.

Also, in a normal year there is an "average" of twenty-two lightning strikes a year. During the summer of 1988 there were more than fifty—more than double the usual number of strikes.

Though called a let burn policy, no federal agency simply allowed all fires to burn at will over the landscape.

The final factor was the wind, which sometimes reached near hurricane force. Wind will drive several fires together and, with a steady source of oxygen, the blazes grow higher. At some critical juncture the fires begin to make their own winds, with hot air from the fires rising rapidly upwards, while new oxygen rushes in from the bottom to fuel the flames which in turn drive the fires to new heights. These winds, coupled with the low humidity, were responsible for the vast acreage that burned and also contributed to the inability of firefighters to contain the flames.

Fires usually burn with uneven intensity, jumping over large patches of forest, leaving behind a patchy mosaic of trees rather than a giant barren moonscape. Photo by George Wuerthner.

A fire usually requires a "ladder" provided by an understory of
smaller trees before it can leap into the crown. Photo by Erwin and
Peggy Bauer.

Of the total park acreage which experienced some burning, less than one percent, or 22,000 acres, experienced the high intensity fires which left little more than ashes.

Due to the tendency of national and local media to focus on the most dramatic and visually exciting aspects of the fires, many people were given the impression that nearly all of Yellowstone National Park was left in cinders. However, a substantial portion of the park was not even touched by fires, and all of the major park attractions such as the Grand Canyon of the Yellowstone, the Old Faithful Geyser Basin, Mammoth Hot Springs and other sites were bypassed by the flames.

Within the 13 million acre Greater Yellowstone area, roughly 1.38 million acres (early estimates) were inside the burn perimeter. This includes the acreage burned on surrounding National Forest lands. Of this, 1 million acres or less were within the park borders. (At the time of this writing park researchers have yet to complete a final mapping of the fire's perimeter, however, readers should bear in mind that park officials believe these figures may be revised downward as much as fifty percent once the inventory is completed.) It must be pointed out that not every acre within the burn perimeter was actually swept by flames. Instead, fires skip and jump over large areas of forest and meadow, very often without even singeing a branch or blade of grass. Of the million acres or less "burned" inside the park, less than half—some 440,000 acres (or twenty percent of the total park acreage)—were actually touched by flames. At least half of these acres (220,000) were only lightly scorched. Of the total park acreage which experienced some burning, less than one percent, or 22,000 acres, experienced the high intensity fires which left little more than ashes. Indeed, once the smoke cleared with the fall rain and snow, many park visitors were astonished to find how much of Yellowstone was untouched or merely singed by the largest fires on record in this region.

Headlines that Yellowstone was in "ashes" helped mislead much of the nation into thinking that all of Yellowstone was reduced to cinders.

Opposite page:
Fresh snow in a mature lodgepole pine forest near Old Faithful. The understory of smaller lodgepole pine indicates that the canopy has been opened to additional sunlight, most likely as a result of pine beetle infestation sometime in the recent past. Photo by George Wuerthner.

ECOLOGICAL SETTING

WHEN the first explorers entered Yellowstone Park, they found a landscape that looked substantially different from the one which tourists see today. Repeated fires had left large areas of the park in the early stages of forest regeneration. Meadow areas were larger, and many south-facing hillsides were spotted with just a few trees, or were entirely barren. Sagebrush, a fire intolerant species, was far less common than at present, while aspen, a fire dependent species, flourished.

There has been a progressive shift since the time of the early Yellowstone explorers to more advanced stages of plant succession. This is due partly to fire suppression at lower elevations, as well as to the fact that intervals between fires at the higher elevations are typically long.

The well watered high elevation of the Yellowstone Plateau is ideal for forest growth. The nearly continuous forest provides a giant fuel supply which is one reason fires tend to be large, though infrequent, events. Looking south from Dunraven Pass to Mt. Sheridan and Tetons. Photo by George Wuerthner.

Prior to the 1988 summer fires, most of Yellowstone's lodgepole pine forests could be characterized as even-aged stands between 100-150 years old which established themselves after the last major Yellowstone fires of a century or more ago. At higher elevations, lodgepole pines may be two hundred or more years in age.

Since the vast majority of the Yellowstone Plateau is above 8,000 feet and nearly continuously covered with dense, even-aged mature lodgepole pine, it is not surprising that—given the right conditions—forest fires there are capable of burning sizeable acreages with great intensity. The ideal conditions for such fires are only infrequently met, however, for several reasons. First, the generally cold temperatures at such high elevations means annual growth rates are comparatively slow. It may require more than a hundred years for a lodgepole pine to reach a diameter of eight inches! The slow growth means the amount of biomass produced each year is relatively small. This is another way of saying that fuel accumulates slowly. In addition, the average precipitation at higher elevations in the park is between 30-80 inches annually and it is usually too wet for fires to cover large acreages. Nevertheless, as a result of the longer interval without fuel-reducing fires, accumulations of dead litter are greater, so that once the inevitable fire comes, it is more likely to be of great intensity.

An uncrowded forest, thinned by light periodic fires is more likely to be a healthy forest . . .

As a contrast, the northern portion of the park along the lower Yellowstone River valley between Gardiner and the Lamar Valley is much drier. Ten inches is the annual precipitation at Gardiner, Montana. (For comparison, Tucson, Arizona averages between 12-14 inches per year.) Summer temperatures are much warmer than on the central plateau and during most winters there is little or no snow cover. This is the prime winter range for many of

The northern portion of Yellowstone park is much lower and drier. It is dominated by grasslands, sagebrush and occasional groves of aspen and Douglas fir. Prior to fire suppression fires burned frequently—every 20-40 years. Photo by George Wuerthner.

Yellowstone's big game herds and it is covered by drought resistant grasses and shrubs like sagebrush, with occasional groves of aspen and Douglas fir tucked into the slightly wetter pockets and draws. The drier nature of this area results in higher fire frequency—an average of 20-30 years between burns. Fires are less intense, however, because fuel accumulations remain low.

Although the amount of annual precipitation is important in determining fire frequency, the pattern of yearly precipitation is probably of greater influence. The ten inches of precipitation that falls on Gardiner at the north entrance of Yellowstone is not evenly distributed throughout the year. Rather, most of it falls as snow in the winter and as late spring rains. Except for an occasional thundershower, summers are exceptionally dry. The same generalization can be made for most of the park: though the amount of precipitation that falls on an area within the park varies with elevation, in all areas most of the moisture comes between late fall and early spring. Summer drought is common everywhere in the park.

The lack of summer precipitation has important implications for the rate at which dead organic matter decomposes. Unlike the warm, moist summer climate experienced by much of the eastern United States—which favors decomposition of matter by soil bacteria and fungi—the general aridity of the West, often combined with cool temperatures at higher elevations, inhibits the growth of these biodecomposers. In the West, dead branches and downed timber do not rot—they accumulate, sometimes for centuries. As a result of the inevitable build-up of litter on the forest floor, a significant proportion of the available nutrients within the ecosystem are locked up and become increasingly unavailable for new plant growth. Many western forests begin to "starve."

Weak from nutrient shortages, and often suffering from overcrowding as well, the forest is increasingly susceptible to disease and insect outbreaks. It is more than coincidental that outbreaks of pine beetle, spruce budworm and other forest pathogens have increased substantially since fire suppression was instituted widely.

The Yellowstone River near Gardiner, Montana receives less than ten inches of precipitation a year—less than Tucson, Arizona. In the past, prior to fire suppression, blazes were fairly common but of a low intensity, barely singeing grasses and shrubs. Photo by George Wuerthner.

Duff and litter consisting of dead branches, fallen pine needles, and pine cones covers the forest floor and provides the fuel for light fires. Here, a serotinous lodgepole pine cone has been opened by the heat of a fire. Photo by George Wuerthner.

Pine beetles have killed some of the trees in this lodgepole pine stand. By thinning the stand, and reducing competition between individual trees, the survivors grow faster and are stronger. Pine beetles, like fire, make the forest healthier. The dead trees fall and provide fuels for subsequent fires which help ensure the lodgepole pines' dominance on a site. Photo by George Wuerthner.

In the arid West, it is fire, not bacteria and fungi, that is the primary agent responsible for breaking down dead organic matter and recycling nutrients back into the soil. Fire releases energy and nutrients rapidly, sending a "pulse" throughout the ecosystem. It is the repetition of these pulses of energy, not the influence of a single event, which maintains the ecosystem's stability.

Recycling of nutrients by fire is not the only ecological role this environmental agent plays in western forest ecosystems. Fires also help thin forests by killing some but not all trees within a burn perimeter. Thinning reduces competition for both nutrients and light among the remaining trees which results in healthier forests. When viewed in this light, fires can be seen as a friend, not an enemy of the forest. Like the predator that keeps its prey populations in balance, fire maintains vegetative communities in a healthy, dynamic relationship with the limited resources available to them.

As a rule, areas recently burned will not carry a fire. Hence these past burns are natural fire breaks. They help to reduce the fire hazard and future suppression costs. Nonetheless, there are exceptions and 1988 was one such year where unusual fire conditions pushed blazes through several recent burns that had just begun to regenerate.

Periodic fires also help to maintain some meadows. Though light, "cool" burns will remove most of the aboveground stalks and stems of grasses and shrubs, the insulative soil protects the roots, and in spring new plants sprout forth. However, most tree species lack the ability to sprout from roots (aspen is one important exception), and frequent fires can prevent invasion of meadows by trees. Visitors who happily gaze upon the open horizon provided by Yellowstone's meadows and grasslands are admiring the work of fire.

Other positive influences associated with fire include the creation or rejuvenation of wildlife habitat, the effective reduction of forest pathogens such as rust and fungi

by the fires' smoke; and the baking of upper soil layers which sometimes kills root rots and can destroy allelopathic chemicals which inhibit the germination and growth of plant seeds. Wildfires may even be responsible for accelerating soil development. I found many boulders cracked by heat or that had small slivers and chips flaked off. These exposed surfaces and smaller rock pieces will break down more rapidly into the finer particles necessary for soil development. Repeated numerous times over thousands of years, the heating and cracking of rocks due to forest fires may be a significant factor in the creation of new soil.

Like the predator that keeps its prey populations in balance, fire maintains vegetative communities in a healthy, dynamic relationship with the limited resources available to them.

However, most of these benefits cannot be realized unless a significant acreage burns per century. Since most fires tend to burn little or no acreage, many fire researchers conclude that it is crucial that large fires be tolerated. Only large blazes are, ecologically speaking, significant. This is one reason why researchers feel prescribed burns (fires purposely ignited under certain "prescribed" conditions to reduce fuel loads) are not a practical alternative to a natural burn policy for a large area like the Yellowstone Plateau. Prescribed burn may be useful for achieving fuel reductions in very small, site specific areas like the woodlands surrounding park developments or near bordering towns, but to eliminate the fuel loading over a massive area such as the Greater Yellowstone—where episodic fires are the rule—would require a prescribed burn program involving tens of thousands of acres each year.

The scarred trunks of this aspen grove are the result of heavy browsing by elk. Fire will likely rejuvenate many of the park's aspen groves since aspen sprouts suckers or shoots from its roots if fire reduces the aboveground canopy. Photo by George Wuerthner.

But even if one disagreed with the opinion of researchers about the ecological need for large fires, the question remains: Can humans really prevent major conflagrations from occurring? Many people have accused the Park Service of some kind of perverse, blind allegiance to "naturalness," and thus the let burn policy. They say that this impractical, irrational philosophy was the root of the great evil that visited the Park in 1988. However, there is a great deal of scientific evidence to suggest that wildfire within the Yellowstone ecosystem is absolutely unavoidable and at best only the timing and intensity of the inevitable blazes can be changed by humans. All out suppression, particularly in a drought year, is mere illusion.

Despite the biggest fire fighting effort ever attempted in United States history, the fires could not be controlled until the weather changed . . .

Heat from passing fires will often crack or flake slivers of rock from boulders. Repeated over and over again by frequent fires, over geological time fires may significantly contribute to soil development. Photo by George Wuerthner.

To blame the park's let burn policies for the severity of the fires is to ignore the other 2.6 million acres which burned elsewhere in the West and Alaska during the summer of 1988. Even within Yellowstone, the decision to suppress all fires began on July 15th when less than 8,600 acres had been charred. More than twenty fires which began after this date were fought by immediate suppression, and ten others which had begun burning prior to the 15th were attacked and fire fighting efforts were directed at containment and suppression. Despite the biggest fire fighting effort ever attempted in United States history, the fires could not be controlled until the weather changed and storm clouds finally brought rain and snow to the area.

Some attribute the marked lack of success at suppression to an abnormal build-up of fuels due to past suppression efforts. Certainly, as a rule, suppression has contributed to greater than normal fuel accumulations in many areas of the West, but there is still a debate about whether fire suppression has really interfered with natural fire cycles at the higher elevations in Yellowstone. Due to the inaccessibility of much of the backcountry, fire suppression has probably been successful only for thirty or forty years at most. Since the natural interval between major fires in these higher elevations is fairly long—an estimated 200-400 years—it is likely that the park's past suppression policies contributed little or only moderately to higher fuel accumulations in these specific forests.

From an ecologist's perspective it is the suppression of fires, not the fires themselves, which is destructive. Wildfires are the dominant driving force behind the Yellowstone ecosystem, as rain is to the tropical rainforests.

Fires are less frequent in Yellowstone's lodgepole pine forests than elsewhere because most of the park's timber stands lack any kind of shrub layer to carry a fire. The understory of most park lodgepole pine forests is surprisingly barren. These forests are in fact often referred to by biologists as "biological deserts." In many places, 85 percent of the forest floor is bare dirt, with only a light litter of pine needles and branches. Even if a fire starts in these forests, it merely creeps along the ground and seldom develops into a large crown fire. It is no wonder that Yellowstone's lodgepole forests have a reputation as "asbestos" forests.

However, if there are no fires for several hundred years, a sub-canopy of shade tolerant tree species such as subalpine fir and Englemann spruce will usually develop beneath the overstory of older lodgepole pine. Since the fir and the spruce do not self-prune (in other words, drop their lower branches) and are also highly flammable, they provide a perfect "ladder" for fires to climb into the higher lodgepole canopy. A creeping ground fire can reach the lower fir and spruce branches and then burn up to the lower limbs of the lodgepole trees. Once the flames have gotten this far, it is quite possible that the fire will "crown out," and rocket to the very top of the forest canopy.

Typically, the only time ecologically significant fires occur in the
high, wet forests of the Yellowstone Plateau is under conditions of
severe drought. Photo by Jim Peaco/NPS.

Opposite page:
A big fire releases the energy equivalent of a small atomic bomb
every 5-15 minutes. Photo by Jim Peaco/NPS.

Smoky sky and trumpeter swan. Photo by Erwin and Peggy Bauer.

Opposite:
Elk in the Madison River under a smoky sunset. Photo by Erwin and Peggy Bauer.

Small mammals like this red squirrel can usually find refuge from the flames by hiding in underground burrows where soil protects them from heat. Photo by Erwin and Peggy Bauer.

Bison in charred forest. Photo by Erwin and Peggy Bauer.

A cow elk nurses a calf unconcerned by the fires blazing around them. Photo by Erwin and Peggy Bauer.

The fires of 1988 should stimulate the rejuvenation and improve the nutritional quality of willows, one of the major foods of moose. Photo by Bob Gress.

Fires seldom burn a forest into ashes, rather, many snags remain as potential homes for cavity-nesting birds like bluebirds and woodpeckers. In addition, over a period of years, the dead trees fall into waterways, providing structural support for streambanks slowing erosion and creating new habitat for trout. Photo by George Wuerthner.

ECOLOGICAL FACTORS

Fire is a common and frequent element in the ecological setting of the Rockies; thus, it is not surprising that many plants and animals are specifically adapted to its periodic occurrence. A plant or animal is successfully adapted to

fire if it is able to leave behind progeny—for example, seeds in the soil—though the adult individual, a tree for example, may not necessarily survive the fire itself.

No species and certainly no individual can be completely prepared for the innumerable, variable events and conditions which may threaten its survival during its life. Thus, each species has evolved a specific set of adaptations which works best most of the time under the kinds of conditions it is most likely to encounter. Scientists call these adaptations "ecological strategies." Among the vegetative communities of the fire-influenced West, different plants have evolved a variety of ecological strategies. Douglas fir, for example, is a common tree fringing the grasslands found at the drier lower elevation areas in the northern part of the park. Fire occurs here on the average of every 30-60 years; thus, Douglas fir must be able to tolerate fairly frequent, periodic fires. Many Douglas fir trees live up to 400 years or more, so some individuals survive multiple reoccurrences of fire. The strategy of Douglas fir is to survive the fires so that old mature individuals can reseed the burned-over landscape to ensure a new generation of the species. Among its adaptations is thick bark on the mature trees which makes them relatively impervious to low intensity fires. In addition, Douglas fir is self-pruning. Small fires burning through the duff and litter on the forest floor are thus unable to "ladder" into the crown of the tree by burning up through branches close to the ground. However, if fires are absent for too long a period of time, a dense thicket of young Douglas fir develops, providing the means for fire to reach the tops of the trees.

Though the old mature Douglas fir are seldom harmed by small fires, young Douglas fir are thin-barked and thus more likely to die from any fire—even a light burn. Fire thins the stands, reducing competition among the survivors and assuring adequate light, nutrients and water for the new crop of seedlings which is likely to spring up in the wake of the flames.

While Douglas fir attempts to survive the flames, the thin-barked aspen, another species common to the dry northern part of the park, seldom survives even a moderately hot fire. In addition, aspen seeds have very precise germination requirements which can seldom be met anyplace in the West. Even if a few mature trees do survive the flames, the likelihood of a new grove estab-

lishing itself from seeds is very, very remote. Obviously, aspen has another means of regeneration, for if it did not, it would soon be lost from the flora. Fire seldom destroys aspen root stocks, and even if the aboveground boles are eliminated, the plant responds by sending up literally thousands of stems, or "suckers", from its roots. As many as 60,000 suckers per acre have been counted in a disturbed aspen grove. Since these suckers can draw resources from the established root system, they can

The thick-barked Douglas fir in the foreground has resisted the flames which now consume the thin-barked lodgepole pine in the background. Photo by George Wuerthner.

Fire typically does not kill all trees in a stand. Here only the younger Douglas fir were killed while the more mature trees, protected by thick bark, survived the blazes intact. Photo by George Wuerthner.

quickly outcompete seedlings from other tree species which must first develop adequate root systems before spending limited resources on the growth of a trunk. As a result, aspen easily dominates a site following fire, and if natural disturbances continue to occur, aspen will remain for generations on the same general site.

Some scientists speculate that nearly all aspen groves were established during a wetter, cooler climatic regime which existed at the close of the Ice Age 10,000 years ago, and that most of these groves have maintained themselves since then by sucker regeneration, not by seed germination and growth. In this sense, some Rocky Mountain aspen groves may be among the oldest living things on Earth.

Aspen not only provide beautiful splashes of autumn gold in an otherwise green coniferous forest, they are also ecologically important to many animals. Because the soils under an aspen grove are seldom acidic, as they are under a coniferous forest, a richer shrub and flower flora can exist in their understory. Grazing and browsing

Aspen are an important ecological and aesthetic feature of Yellowstone Park. Most aspen regeneration occurs after wildfire removes the aboveground boles and thus stimulates the production of suckers or new shoots from the roots. Photo by George Wuerthner.

species like elk are drawn to these groves for the highly nutritious foods growing there. In addition, elk will even eat aspen bark in times of stress, and many of the lower boles of aspen in the Park are blackened by scar tissue which has grown up and discourages further elk browsing.

Fire releases energy and nutrients rapidly, sending a "pulse" throughout the ecosystem.

Aspen is also an important food for beaver. The beaver eat the bark and inner cambium layer of the tree. They also use the easily chewed branches for construction of dams and lodges. The numerous beaver dams which once existed in the park served as important check dams, slowing sedimentation in major rivers. The beaver ponds also provided an opportunity for the cold waters to warm and thus become more productive. Higher trout populations were among the results of higher levels of beaver activity. Once a colony of beavers had exhausted its local aspen supply, the site was abandoned and the ponds gradually filled in—creating wet meadows and ideal habitat for succulent plants sought by elk, grizzlies, and other animals.

Aspen grows rapidly, but its vigor declines after 80-100 years. Most of the groves in Yellowstone were at or past this critical age in 1988. Since fire suppression has been most successful in the northern part of the park, and since fires have burned here historically on the average of once every 20-25 years, the impact of suppression has been particularly hard on the park's aspen communities. In addition, since much of the northern portion of the park is important winter range for elk, bison, antelope and other animals, each winter there is a significant reduction in grass and other plants which might help to carry a fire. As a result of this and the suppression of the few fires which have started, there has been little disturbance to stimulate sucker regeneration. The suckers that do occasionally sprout are quickly eaten by the park's numerous elk herds. Prior to the fires of 1988, most of the park's aspen groves were on the decline and even threatened with local extinction. One anticipated result of this summer's fires will be the stimulation of sucker development in burned aspen groves, which may succeed in establishing a new generation of trees.

Aspen are not the only species which sprout from roots after a fire. Many species of willows have the same ability. Due to fire suppression as well as insect damage

Re-growth after a fire is rapid as the influx of ash, nutrients, light, and water stimulates the growth of many plants like the willows seen here sprouting from charred stumps. Photo by George Wuerthner.

Old beaver ponds often fill in to become wet meadows, which are a favorite foraging area for many wildlife species including grizzly bear. Photo by George Wuerthner.

and heavy browsing by moose, elk and other ungulates, Yellowstone's willow stands had declined in general height and area. Wildfire usually rejuvenates willow stands, and it is anticipated that willows will experience a revitalization on burned sites.

Rabbitbrush, a common and edible shrub in the northern part of the park, is also a root sprouter, as are many flowering plants like arnica and lupine. Most perennial grasses sprout new shoots readily after a fire. Since fuel accumulations are usually quite low in such dry, open grassland habitats, fires typically race through rather quickly and little heat penetrates deeply into the soil where it could kill root stocks. With the elimination of dead material, the release of nutrients, and the increased availability of light and water in the burned patches, grasslands typically respond quickly and regrowth is almost immediate. Much of the northern part of the park was burned by this kind of light, quick moving fire and will sport a new lush growth of grasses by the spring of 1989.

Much of the northern part of the park was burned by this kind of light, quick moving fire and will sport a new lush growth of grasses by the spring of 1989.

Unlike the many low elevation species that regenerate via root sprouting, plants at higher elevations of the park tend to rely more on seeds to maintain the species. This is because the less frequent, but more intense fires that occur in these areas are more likely to burn hot and can kill most or all of the trees outright.

The most abundant tree species in Yellowstone, lodgepole pine, makes up nearly 80 percent of all forest cover in the park and forms nearly pure stands—primarily the result of regeneration after past fires. Lodgepole is ideally adapted to long-interval, but periodic perturbations. Mature lodgepole produces two kinds of cones—open and serotinous. Open cones shed seed when the cone reaches maturity. Nearly every year, some seeds are shed from the tree. Serotinous cones, on the other hand, are sealed closed by a resin coating which requires temperatures of at least 113 degrees before they will open. Such temperatures never occur on the high, cool Yellowstone Plateau except during a fire. These cones remain on the tree unopened for years and provide an abundant seed source that scatters over the ground within days of the passage of a fire. The ratio of serotinous to non-serotinous cones in any lodgepole population seems to be related to the frequency of fire. If fires are common, the serotinous cones will dominate; if fires are rare, open cones are more common.

Wildfires cannot destroy Yellowstone; misguided attempts to suppress all fires can.

The ability of lodgepole pine to rapidly reseed an area after a fire gives it an immense advantage over competing conifers whose seeds must be blown onto the site from nearby seed sources—if they even exist. Once established, a young lodgepole seedling grows very rapidly and matures early. Some lodgepole pine can produce seed-bearing cones when they are five years old. Other Yellowstone forest species like sub-alpine fir may not produce mature cones until they are fifty plus years in age. As a further adaptation, serotiny is not expressed until a tree is between 30-60 years of age. This allows young, but cone producing, lodgepole to maximize restocking of an area during the early development and regeneration of a stand.

The periodic repetition of wildfires tends to perpetuate lodgepole pine since stands of the more shade-tolerant climax species, like subalpine fir and Engelmann spruce, seldom get the opportunity to mature and produce seeds. In the instances where a lodgepole stand does not burn for a hundred or more years, subalpine fir and spruce will begin to grow up in the understory, and will eventually come to dominate the site. Only so long as there is no subsequent disturbance of the forest—such as fire, wind storm, or disease—will the shade-tolerant species remain. Of course, this is, in a sense, what the lodgepole pine is "counting on." Sub-alpine fir and Engelmann spruce are unable to tolerate fire and are not adapted to quickly re-colonize an opened, disturbed site—as the pine is. These two species do not self-prune (as do Douglas fir and lodgepole) and both are extremely flammable—even when green. In fact, Indians often lit a fir just to see it flare up. The show was rather like a fireworks display without the gunpowder. Because of their fire intolerance, fir and spruce are usually confined to places that do not burn frequently: streamsides, wet meadows, near timberline. Episodic, large fires as witnessed in Yellowstone during the summer of 1988 are probably the chief factor contributing to the continued reign of lodgepole pine in the Yellowstone ecosystem.

If another fire does not sweep through to thin it, a mature lodgepole pine stand eventually begins to break up due to wind throw (that is, the breaking of branches and falling of trees due to wind storms) and insect attacks.

New grass sprouts from fallen timber less than two weeks after the North Fork Fire raced through this area by Madison Junction. Photo by George Wuerthner.

The serotinous cones of lodgepole pine, seen here, open upon heating by fire, thus shedding seed over recently burned ground. Photo by George Wuerthner.

One of the major insect "predators" of mature lodgepole pine is the mountain pine beetle. The pine beetle selectively attacks dense, crowded, mature lodgepole pine stands—stands weakened by intense competition. The pine beetle normally attacks trees that are larger than eight inches in diameter and that grow at elevations of less than 9,000 feet. The beetle bores its way through the lodgepole's bark and lays its eggs in the inner cambium—the living cell layer just beneath the bark which is the conduit for nutrients and water flowing between the roots and the foliage in the tree crown. As the eggs hatch, the larvae eat away at this cambium layer and eventually girdle the tree, cutting off the flow of water and nutrients. The ultimate result is the death of the tree. A healthy pine tree can expel the beetle larvae before significant damage is done, unlike the weakened, older specimens. An uncrowded forest, thinned by light periodic fires is more likely to be a healthy forest, and thus less susceptible to a killing infestation of mountain pine beetles.

Since lodgepole pine can easily outcompete all other species for dominance after a fire, it is possible to suggest that lodgepole pine may actually "welcome" fire.

But from the perspective of the species, even death caused by the pine beetle is not really a loss. As trees die, the forest canopy opens up and allows light to reach the forest floor, making for more suitable growing conditions for young lodgepole pine. In addition, the dead and dying trees provide an ideal fuel source for a fire, should an ignition occur. Since lodgepole pine can easily outcompete all other species for dominance after a fire, it is possible to suggest that lodgepole pine may actually "welcome" fire.

Over time lodgepole pine as well as other trees will slowly invade a meadow. Periodic fire not only opens up and thins a forest, keeping it healthier, but it also helps to maintain many of the park's meadows. Photo by George Wuerthner.

Elk grazes in lush meadow immediately next to blackened forest. Photo by Erwin and Peggy Bauer.

The woman in this photo gives scale to the mature lodgepole pine stand which has an understory of subalpine fir. It takes several hundred years for a lodgepole stand to develop such understory characteristics. The highly flammable fir provides a "ladder" which allows fires to climb up into the canopy. Photo by George Wuerthner.

The impact of fire on wildlife is usually minimal, and Smokey the Bear posters which show a host of terrorized animals fleeing a wall of flames is more fiction than fact. The fire itself will probably have a positive effect on the diversity and numbers of wildlife species. Wildfire usually leaves a mosaic pattern of burning, where some areas are charred, others only lightly burned, and still others left untouched. This "patchy" landscape means that there is more diversity of habitat, and thus more places for different kinds of plant and animal species to find a suitable living environment.

One Yellowstone researcher found that following fire there is a gradual increase in plant, bird and mammal species until a maximum number is reached about 25 years later. Once the lodgepole pine canopy closes—at about 40-50 years following a fire—there is a precipitous decline in diversity. From the 25 year peak, diversity of both plants and animals plummets by 65 percent. Eliminated are approximately fifty plant species, eight to ten bird species and eight small mammal species. The resulting low number of species is maintained until a lodgepole forest reaches approximately 300 years in age, when disease, insect attack, and wind throw begins to break up the closed canopy and allows for slightly greater species diversity.

The impact of fire on wildlife is usually minimal and Smokey the Bear posters which show a host of terrorized animals fleeing a wall of flames is more fiction than fact.

Immediately after a fire, standing dead trees are attacked by round-headed woodborers—a beetle which is attracted by smoke to recently burned areas. The high beetle population in turn attracts an unusually high number of woodpeckers, particularly northern three-toed woodpeckers, whose numbers increase rapidly after a fire in response to the higher beetle numbers. Northern three-toed woodpecker populations tap this temporary food source for two to five years before they move on to another recently burned area. During their brief residence in the burned area they excavate numerous cavities that later provide nest sites for birds like the mountain bluebird, black-capped chickadee, yellow-bellied sapsucker, and tree swallow. The dead snags remain as important nest habitat for 40-50 years, until the new generation of lodgepole pine has grown tall enough to close the forest canopy. All cavity nesting birds will have vanished by this stage in the forest's succession.

Changes in plant diversity, density, and the sprouting of new vegetation (willows and aspen, for example) will also provide new or expanded habitat for a wide variety of birds including warblers and sparrows. However, species like the goshawk that are dependent upon old growth timber can be expected to decline in certain areas. Nevertheless, due to the vast size of Yellowstone and the tremendous acreage of untouched habitat, the loss of

Only 254 large mammals were killed by the fires and most died from suffocation. Photo by Linda Best.

Large mammals like this bison can walk away from most fires, and the shaggy beasts will focus their grazing on the new growth that will arrive in the spring. Photo by George Wuerthner.

some old stands should not be deleterious to the overall population of these birds or other old growth dependent species.

... the most stressful behavior I observed in several groups of elk was caused not by the fires, but by the loud noise of the helicopters ...

Small mammals typically seek shelter from fires in burrows underground. Soil is an excellent insulator and in most cases the heat of a fire does not penetrate more than an inch or so underground. Though an occasional squirrel or pine marten may be overtaken by a rapidly moving fire, most of the time these animals can outrun the flames or seek shelter in the many patches of unburned timber which usually exist within a fire's perimeter. The mortality that does occur is usually the result of suffocation, not high temperatures or actual burning. The flush of new grasses and shrubs following the fires should provide for an overall increase in small

mammal populations as well as the species diversity of such animals. Typically, four small mammal species can be found in a burned area a year after a fire has passed through. Within twenty-five years, that number has increased to twelve. Diversity declines with the continued growth of the forest, until it reaches a sustained, stable level of from three to five small mammal species.

Most bird species are untroubled by wildfire because under natural conditions fires usually do not occur until after the spring nesting season when the young are able to fly and thus escape the flames.

Large mammals such as elk, deer, bear and bison usually walk away from the flames and most show a surprising lack of concern about nearby fires. Elk and other wildlife were seen repeatedly grazing just beyond a blazing forest. I watched one herd of elk amble through a still burning forest, apparently unconcerned by the flaming timber around them. In fact, the most stressful behavior I observed in several groups of elk was caused not by the fires, but by the loud noise of the helicopters engaged in fire suppression efforts. Each time a chopper came near, the elk tensed and several bunches made disorganized, frenzied dashes for cover.

Despite the ability of most animals to escape the flames, there are occasions when individuals get trapped by fire and die. The observed casualties from the 1988 fires include five bison, approximately 243 elk, one black bear, two moose and four deer. Cutthroat trout in the Little Firehole River were also killed as a result of the fires, but not from the flames or heat: fire retardant was accidently dropped into the stream.

Though it will be shortlived, the greatest immediate effect the fires will have on wildlife is the loss of big game winter range in the northern part of the park. Approximately eleven percent of the park's winter range burned, and this temporary loss of food, coupled with the drought year's lower plant productivity may result in a higher than average number of deaths the first winter, due to starvation. Though there are some people who insist that the Park Service should feed winter-stressed animals, such a scheme is ill-advised. Not only is artificial feeding very expensive, it tends to keep more animals alive than the land can physically support. In addition, animals are concentrated in feeding areas, and since they continue to feed on natural vegetation as well, severe overgrazing is the frequent outcome.

There is a gradual increase in both plant, bird and mammal species following fire.

Beyond these short-term impacts, the long-term prognosis for most park big game species is positive. The expansion of grasslands will benefit grazers like bighorn sheep and bison, while the re-sprouting and renewed vigor of shrubs like chokecherry, serviceberry, willows and aspen is sure to be a boon to moose and elk. Many scientific studies have documented the preference shown by big game species for browsing and grazing on the tender, more nutritious post-fire growth.

The park's grizzlies are likely to feel little impact from the fires, at least initially. The greatest loss to them will

Like many birds of prey, the great horned owl was able to benefit from the fires by finding prey easier in the burned-over areas. Photo by Erwin and Peggy Bauer.

be the limited mortality of some high elevation whitebark pine, which provides one of the bear's favorite foods. The whitebark pine cones have a large seed, like a pinyon nut, that is high in energy and feasted upon by grizzlies fattening up for the winter. On the positive side of the ledger, the increase in forest patchiness, meadows, and growth of fire-induced plants will probably ultimately result in more food and nutrition for grizzlies. In addition, the potential for significant big game winter die-offs in the first few years following the fires will mean a rich supply of carrion for the bears in the springtime.

The long term prognosis for most park big game species is positive.

Yellowstone's trout fisheries are world famous and there is justifiable concern about the fire's impacts on this resource. The fires notwithstanding, the greatest impact on fish is the result of the drought which dropped stream flows, concentrating all fish in a far smaller amount of habitat, and significantly increasing competition for food, and space. Nevertheless, there are a few short-term negative impacts to fisheries which may result. The most important is sedimentation due to increased erosion of newly bare ground. Although most burned sites were not totally stripped of duff (pine needles, leaves, twigs and other small bits of organic matter that accumulate on the forest floor) or of the important top layer of soil that contains grass and shrub roots, many areas were indeed left with very little protective cover on the ground. Soils will

Far more animals die due to the harshness of winter on the high cold Yellowstone Plateau than are ever killed by fires. Photo by George Wuerthner.

be more easily carried off the land by rain and spring runoff.

Whether erosion resulting from snowmelt becomes a problem will depend largely upon how much snowfall occurs during the next few winters and on the rate of melt in the spring. If snowfall is heavy and spring melt is rapid, or accompanied by heavy rains, erosion could be quite significant in the first year or two following the blazes. The removal by fire of shade-providing trees means that snow will melt and run off earlier and faster than in sites where trees are still standing and still bear their needles. Increased streambank and streambed erosion is the likely secondary result of an earlier, more concentrated run-off period. This means fish spawning areas may receive more unwanted silt, and aquatic insects may decline—also as a result of higher sediment loads in the water.

Fisheries may benefit from the pulse of nutrients that flows into stream systems following large fires.

However, several factors can check erosion after a fire. In light burns only the dead tops of grasses and shrubs are burned away, leaving root systems intact. These roots continue to bind the soil, slowing erosion. In portions of the burn where the forest canopy was only scorched, not consumed, fallen dead needles create a soft matlike covering which also helps prevent erosion. Soon after fires had passed through an area, many trees in the park stood in the center of rust-colored pools—the dead needles each had dropped about themselves.

Further erosion protection is provided when snags topple from wind to form numerous check dams on hillsides. Susceptibility to erosion also decreases rapidly two to three years after a fire, as vegetation recovery brings erosion and sedimentation back to pre-burn levels. Since plant cover increases above even pre-burn levels five

to ten years after a fire, there is often a substantial reduction in erosion—it often dropping below levels that existed prior to a fire.

Fisheries may benefit from from the pulse of nutrients that flows into stream systems following large fires. It is thought that these pulses provide long-term enrichment of aquatic ecosystems. In addition, due to the park's high elevation, most of the waters are exceedingly cold (except for rivers like the Firehole, which are partly fed by large thermal features). The low water temperatures slow the growth of trout as well as the food the trout eat. The burning of dense timber which formerly shaded many smaller streams may mean that water temperatures may rise slightly and thus be more conducive to the growth of fish. At lower elevations outside of the park, streamside shading may be essential for keeping water temperatures below those lethal to trout, but in Yellowstone most waters are below the optimum temperature for trout growth.

As a consequence of the fires, the amount of dead snags which fall into streams will increase. Snags are an important component of fish habitat because they provide cover, and also slow and break up the current, giving fish an opportunity to rest. Some studies have shown that dead snags may provide more than 50 percent of the fish habitat in small to medium size streams. Moreover, since charred snags remain standing for decades, toppling one by one over the years, they provide a continuous long-term source of new fish habitat.

The conclusion of most fire specialists is that the large wildfires were unavoidable.

Animals killed by fire or harsh winters help to feed other park wildlife like this black bear. Photo by Erwin and Peggy Bauer.

In their own way, these snags on Mt. Washburn have their own
aesthetic beauty. Photo by George Wuerthner.

Opposite page:
Though most of the Park appeared blackened as a result of the
1988 fires, frequently the duff and grasses were only lightly singed as
seen here, and thus continued to provide a covering which helps to
prevent soil erosion. Photo by George Wuerthner.

A firefighter set off by glow of fires. Photo by Jeff Henry/NPS.

Helicopters were used to carry firefighters to blazes and to dump water on flames. At a cost of $1700 an hour, helicopter time is one of the major expenses of fighting a fire. Photo by Jim Peaco/NPS.

A firefighter in field. Photo by Paul Fraughton.

Firefighters walk to work. Photo by Paul Fraughton.

Park ranger, Mike Badger, like many park employees switched jobs during the summer of 1988 and donned firefighting gear. Photo by Jeff Henry/NPS.

Firefighters used a foamy mixture of detergent and water to smother flames and coat buildings. Photo by Jim Peaco/NPS.

A tired firefighter. Photo by Jim Peaco/NPS.

Slurry bomber dropping fire retardant on fire. Photo by Paul Fraughton.

Marines, seen here marching out from a fire, as well as the Army, were sent to Yellowstone to help battle the blazes. Photo by George Wuerthner.

Exhausted firefighters sleep at Mammoth. Photo by Jim Peaco/NPS.

Burning logs may hold fire for weeks, allowing winds to revive fires long thought to be contained or suppressed. Photo by Paul Fraughton.

FIRE BEHAVIOR

A forest fire often seems alive. It will often move slowly, sleepily, only grudgingly gaining ground. Yet it can suddenly rear back, driven by powerful winds, and roar down in pulsating power surges that make the suppression efforts of humans seem puny and almost pitifully inadequent. The way in which a fire behaves is influenced greatly by a host of variables such as fuel loading, wind, humidity, terrain, past fire history, and of course, human suppression efforts. On the Yellowstone Plateau, most fires are likely to be creeping burns, even within timbered areas, due to the overall slow build-up of fuels in this specific region. Such a fire produces what is called by fire specialists a "light to moderate burn." Most of the burned areas in the park can be characterized as such. A light burn is one that merely scorches or at most consumes surface litter and duff, but does not alter soils to any depth.

However, if a fire enters into the older forests where spruce and fir provide a ladder for flames to reach the top of the tree canopy, the fire can gallop across the landscape at astonishing speed, especially if driven by high winds. The heat from a wind-driven crown fire creates a

Intense blaze as fire travels along fallen log. Photo by Erwin and Peggy Bauer.

Fire temporarily closes campground. Photo by Jim Peaco/NPS.

rapidly rising column of heated air, which in turn begins to suck in fresh oxygen from outside of the flames. The flow of air into the center of the conflagration fans the burning embers even more. The fire begins to feed on itself, drawing in more air and sending flames ever higher. Such fires produce an audible roar as they blast through the trees. Great sheets of flame will explode from the advancing fire front and leap forward as if thrown by a giant flame thrower. The fire seems to throb and oscillate as if it is alive and can on occasion make remarkable advances of four or five miles in an hour. Yellowstone's Clover-Mist fire ran 14 miles in just four hours, for example. And on "Black Saturday," August 20, flames driven by winds of more than 60 mph charred over 150,000 acres in one day! Bozeman *Chronicle* reporter, Scott McMillion, witnessed a firestorm descending on the Old Faithful complex, and described windblown embers "as big as a man's fist" being tossed through the air, and bursting into flames on impact.

A forest fire often seems alive.

The winds generated by such firestorms can literally topple trees before the flames ever reach them. Several times this summer the right conditions for a firestorm developed and the resulting sight was an awesome spectacle. In fact, the amount of power released every ten to fifteen minutes by a swirling firestorm is equivalent to the explosion of a small atomic bomb.

---

*. . . flames driven by higher than 60 mph
winds charred over 150,000 acres in one day!*

Under these extreme conditions, human fire suppression efforts are totally ineffective. Once a fire reaches these enormous proportions, it is not only impossible to contain, it is completely foolhardy for anyone to move or be placed in front of the advancing wave of flames. Instances have been documented where intense fires have thrown firebrands as much as ten miles in advance of a fire's front. In Yellowstone there were times when sparks were setting off ignitions a mile or more ahead of the main line of flames. No human effort—no matter how bold or powerful—can stop such a force. The narrow dirt pathways scraped by bulldozers, not to mention the insignificant, one-foot wide firelines dug by firefighters, can be jumped by these speeding fires in a matter of moments. The people who complained that the Yellowstone fires could have been contained if more bulldozer lines had been built do not realize how great the power of a major fire can be. When flames and sparks were jumping mile-wide natural barriers such as the Grand Canyon of the Yellowstone, a twenty-foot wide bulldozer swath does not make the least bit of difference.

. . . the amount of power released every ten to fifteen minutes by a swirling firestorm is equivalent to the explosion of a small atomic bomb.

Most fire behavior specialists and seasoned firefighters know that attempting to stop such fires is hopeless. Time and time again records indicate that when severe fire conditions exist, the only time the blazes are brought under control is after the weather changes or the fires run out of fuel. Though in most of these instances the firefighters

. . . embers "as big as a man's fist" were tossed through the air, and burst into flames on impact.

are quick to take credit for quelling the flames, the containment of a fire has more to do with the whims of nature than the actions of humans. Indeed, most fire fighting efforts are (to borrow a line from Shakespeare) "full of sound and fury signifying nothing."

Clover-Mist fire in upper Lamar Valley on July 21st. Photo by Jim Peaco/NPS.

Flaming forest. Photo by Jim Peaco/NPS.

IMPACTS OF THE FIRES

Impacts from fire fighting and recovery
THE Yellowstone forests evolved with fire, but not with D-9 bulldozers.
There is substantial evidence from other areas of the West that suggests that the

longest lasting scars from a fire do not come from the blaze itself, but from the firefighting and "rehabilitation" efforts. For example, the bare mineral soil exposed as a result of fireline construction is far more susceptible to erosion than even moderately burned areas, which are still protected by the duff, roots, and needles that often remain. While even the hottest fires in Yellowstone baked only the first inch or so of soil—having little impact on most soil layers—a bulldozer blade often scrapes away all of the topsoil. It may take centuries for that top organic layer to be replaced.

The Yellowstone forests evolved with fire, but not with D-9 bulldozers.

Rehabilitation projects following a fire can also be less than beneficial to the ecosystem. For example, non-native plant species are often seeded over a burned site. Undesirable weeds may be introduced in the well-meaning but sometimes ill-advised effort to hasten recovery, and rehabilitation becomes just one more disruption to the natural plant communities. (Fires can also hasten the spread of

weeds since bare mineral soils are easily colonized by such pioneering species.)

When flames and sparks were jumping mile-wide natural barriers such as the Grand Canyon of the Yellowstone, a twenty-foot wide bulldozer swath does not make the least bit of difference.

Other impacts from fire fighting include the dumping of fire retardant into streams. The retardant is actually just fertilizer—a nutrient that in small doses would enrich the aquatic habitat—but in concentrated doses it can kill fish and other organisms.

Finally, if suppression efforts are successful, the result is unburned fuel that will only contribute to a hotter, more extensive fire in the future. Fortunately, due to the desire of Yellowstone Park officials and many firefighters to preserve a natural appearing landscape, all of these impacts were kept to a minimum.

Bulldozer lines and other traditional fire breaks are useless against wind-driven fires. As seen here, the fire easily jumped a dozer line. Photo by George Wuerthner.

The scars from bulldozer-constructed firelines often last far longer than any impacts to the ecosystem resulting from the actual fires. Photo by Jim Peaco/NPS.

IMPACTS OF FIRES ON HUMANS

One of the most common effects the Yellowstone fires had on the human population was thick and persistent smoke. During the latter part of August and early September, smoke became a near daily feature of the park and of neighboring communities. It obscured scenic views and created potential health hazards, particularly to those with respiratory problems. For everyone, the smoke caused eyes to water and made breathing unpleasant. The problem was compounded by temperature inversions, a common weather phenomenon in valleys of the West. On still, cool nights, cold air drains down slopes. The dense cool air collects in valley bottoms and basins, pushing the warmer air up, and creating a situation where the layer of warm air traps the cold air beneath. Any smoke, dust, traffic fumes, etc. is held beneath the ceiling of warm air. An inversion acts to dampen fires because there is very little air movement. The fires will smolder, and smoke will lie low until daytime heating breaks the inversion (this may not occur until mid-afternoon). The fires are then revived by a flush of fresh air.

As annoying as smoke may be, it must be realized that without fire—and the accompanying smoke—fuels will continue to accumulate. Smoke is one of those things that probably should be tolerated temporarily for the sake of long-term safety and health. Thankfully, most smoke is readily dispersed in the summer by winds and thermal convection currents, and large, smoke-creating fires of the kind that occurred in Yellowstone in 1988 are relatively uncommon. Most years, smoke is not likely to be a significant problem.

The 1988 fire season officially started in Yellowstone National Park on May 24th when lightning struck a tree in the Lamar Valley.

Though the smoke made breathing an unpleasant experience for many residents near the park, its impacts went beyond personal health. The economic well-being of gateway communities was affected as well. As a result of misinformed, misleading press coverage, which implied

After a fire, plants like the pink fireweed in this picture, will quickly spread over large acreages not only providing a beautiful visual dis-play, but also helping to hold down soil erosion. Photo by George Wuerthner.

Temperature inversions where warm air traps colder air and smoke in mountain valleys were common this summer, contributing to air pollution problems for residents of the park and near-by communi-ties. Most inversions break up in the afternoon as the atmosphere heats up. Photo by Jim Peaco/NPS.

that Yellowstone Park was in ashes, tourist visitation dropped by an estimated 400,000 visitors or about 16 percent of expected. Normally the park receives 2.5 million tourists per year. That drop in visitation translated into notable losses for many businesses, although the impact varied from area to area and business to business. Some out-fitters lost their entire fall hunting incomes due to cancel-lations by customers. Even when customers still opted to honor their reservations, in some cases the nearby national forest lands (where most hunting occurs—hunting is not allowed in Yellowstone Park) were temporarily closed due to the potential fire danger.

. . . a virtual army of firefighters—ten thousand of them—converged on the park, along with 229 pumper trucks, and 57 helicopters.

Despite these losses, some establishments did a brisk business in supplying the army of firefighters with every-thing from motel space to food. For many establishments, the summer fires were a gold mine that provided an unexpected boom, helping to mitigate the loss of tourist dollars. In addition, once the smoke cleared in September, visitation actually increased in October some 39 percent over previous years, as curious on-lookers came to the park to see for themselves what had happened.

Before the fires were quenched more than $120 million had been spent, but given their magnitude the fires caused a surprisingly small amount of damage to property and life.

Although the loss of property was surprisingly low given the size and extent of the fires, a few outlying cabins both in and outside of the park were lost. The federal government made every effort to provide fire pro-tection to personal and public property, but in a few instances the flames were too dangerous to risk the loss of a firefighter's life for the sake of a building. It is possible

Much of the firefighting effort and a great percentage of the cost was spent attempting to protect park developments and nearby communities like Cooke City, pictured here, from the flames. Photo by Jim Peaco/NPS.

enough energy is put into the effort. However, it is also the best that can be hoped for when one is dealing with large fire complexes that are impossible to control or contain. Only when the weather changes are human control efforts likely to have any affect on wildfires in general.

Such a fire summer may come only once during the course of a human lifetime . . .

to argue that there is an inherent risk associated with locating one's home in the forested portions of the West. Where fire is more or less an inevitable natural event, it is an invitation to disaster to build there. Constructing one's home in a heavily-forested mountain valley such as Cooke City at the northeast entrance to the park is rather like placing a house on a flood plain. Fires will not sweep the forest every summer, nor will a flood deluge an entire river bottom each year, but those who build their homes in such places are tempting fate.

The actual flames which nearly engulfed these two communities were the result of "back fires" purposely set by firefighters.

The final impact of the fires on humans was the amount of money spent fighting them. More than $120 million went into the park fires at last count and the bills are still coming in. Was it necessary to spend this amount? It depends on your basic assumptions about fire. If one does not necessarily feel that fires are "destructive," or are at least a necessary ecological force, then far too much money was spent trying to suppress the fires—which as has been seen is a vain attempt.

A more rational approach to fire suppression would have been to direct all money and man-power to protection of communities like Cooke City and park developments like Grant Village, while allowing the fires to run their course in non-developed areas. Because wildfires do not respect human-imposed political boundaries and burn into areas where fires are undesirable, some fire control is necessary. Fire can be deflected around strategic sites like Old Faithful, or human communities like Cooke City, if

In spite of the largest fires in park history, life went on as usual for many park visitors, such as this fisherman trying his luck on the Firehole River as the forest across the river burns. Photo by George Wuerthner.

The fires of Yellowstone are as much as part of Yellowstone's natural diversity as its famous geological displays. Here Old Faithful Geyser is backed by a smoke plume from the North Fork Fire. Photo by Jim Peaco/NPS.

MESSAGE TO THE READER:

Writing a book about an ecological process like fire is difficult. Nearly as soon as the book is printed, new information is needed to account for unpredictable variables such as human influence, and naturally-occurring successional changes in plants, and weather patterns which will occur in Yellowstone after the 1988 fires. In addition, studies initiated after the fires may result in new interpretations of old concepts and it would be desirable to incorporate these findings into the book. Thus, a good book should follow the example set by ecological processes, and rather than being static, should be flexible and gradually evolve over time. With this in mind, the publisher and myself have agreed to update this title with additional text which modifies or expands upon ideas that future research on the park fires has elucidated. In addition, a photo documentation of regeneration and progressive changes in vegetative communities will be incorporated into future editions of this book.

A firefighter uses a torch to purposely set a "back fire." Back fires are used to reduce fuel, and thus slow or stop the advance of a fire. However, sometimes these plans fail. Photo by Jim Peaco/NPS.

The fires of 1988 became a major tourist attraction in themselves, much as people might flock to see a volcanic eruption. Photo by Paul Fraughton.

Unconcerned by the smoke from wildfires, visitors await the eruption of the Old Faithful geyser. Photo by Jim Peaco/NPS.

Fire charred picnic table. Photo by Paul Fraughton.

Flames threaten Grant Village. Photo by Jim Henry/NPS.

Charred cabin at Old Faithful area. Only a few small structures were burned in the fires of 1988; no large building was destroyed. Photo by Ed Cooper.

Firefighters spray water on the wooden roof of the Mammoth Hotel when Mammoth was threatened by fires in early September. Photo by Jim Peaco/NPS.

In an effort to keep telephone poles from burning, firefighters covered their bases with foil. Photo by Jeff Henry/NPS.

Burned sign for Old Faithful by Madison Junction. Photo by Linda Best.

SUMMARY AND CONCLUSION

IF one examines the historic record, it becomes obvious that much of the West is dominated by frequent small intensity fires occasionally interrupted by infrequent fires that burn extensive acreages. Such a fire summer may come only once during the course of a human lifetime, and may thus seem catastrophic; but in reality such a fire is quite predictable given the climatic and ecological conditions which dominate the Western landscape. These episodic fires provide an explosive pulse of energy and nutrients that powers the ecosystem.

One way to view to these periodic fires is to think of the individual explosions in a car's engine cylinder. Isolated and seen alone, these explosions of gas in the cylinder may seem to be potentially destructive, but if viewed from a distance of space and time, it becomes apparent that these repetitious explosions power the car and under normal circumstances do no harm to the engine. In fact, if one disrupts the timing, the engine will not only run rough, it may cease to run altogether.

The flames of the summer of 1988 did not destroy the park for within the fires were cast the seeds of a new beginning.

Similarly, the fire summers of the kind that was witnessed in Yellowstone during 1988 are really nothing more than the single explosions of the ecosystem's "engine." To suppress these fires, reduce their intensity, or even change their frequency by controlled burning will disrupt the ecological timing and perhaps upset Yellowstone's ecological system. Conditioned as we are to view fires as destructive, the sight of charred tree trunks and blackened soils may seem ugly. Yet if we view the changed landscape with a mind to the ecological forces that have shaped it, there is beauty and inspiration here.

The ecological balance in Yellowstone is not static, but part of a dynamic equilibrium achieved through the interaction of many processes, of which wildfire is one. To try to hold the ecosystem to the status quo is impossible.

A forest is more than trees or any other single component. Rather, it is an interaction of ecological processes—including wildfire—acting upon the ecosystem which happens to include trees but is not limited to them. To preserve the forest, it is necessary to preserve the ecological processes under which that forest evolved. The preservation of Yellowstone requires the preservation of periodic large fires. The flames of the summer of 1988 did not destroy the park, for within the fires were cast the seeds of a new beginning. Yellowstone, born in fire, also lives with fire.

Fires are an essential ecological process in the Yellowstone ecosystem. Forests or sage covered slopes are only one part of the nutrient cycle that maintains the park. In some areas, the next step may be a field of flowers. Yellowstone is not destroyed by fires, only changed. Photo by George Wuerthner.

GLOSSARY OF TERMS

allelopathic — chemicals released by plants into the soil which inhibit the growth of other plant species.

biodecomposers — bacteria, fungi and other organisms which break down organic matter into simpler chemical or organic compounds.

biomass — the organic material produced by living plants and animals.

boles — trunks of trees.

browsing — eating branches of trees and shrubs. Moose are typically browers since they eat willows and other shrubs. Bison are typically grazers—feeding on grasses.

cambium layer — the living tissue inside the bark of a tree which acts as a conduit for the transportation of water and nutrients from the roots into the crown and down to the roots again.

carrion — dead animals eaten as food by scavengers.

climax species — plants which are most likely to develop on a particular site and be able to reproduce indefinitely without a further progression to another species group.

conflagration — any large uncontrollable fire.

crown fire — a fire which jumps into the canopy of a forest and is driven by winds from tree top to tree top.

crown out — a fire that has laddered into the canopy of a forest is said to have crowned out.

duff — the organic layer that covers the top portion of soils.

ecosystem — an area in which energy, nutrients, water, and other biological and geological influences work together and influence each other.

episodic — periodic, large fires.

firebrands — small burning or glowing debris blown before an advancing fire.

fire breaks — natural or man-made lines or areas where fuels are limited or non-existent which thus causes a fire to die or slow.

fire complex — when several small fires unite to create one large burn covering thousands of acres.

fire scars — if burned by a fire, scar tissue develops on the tree and leaves a record of that particular burn. Scientists can examine fire scars and determine when and how many fires occurred during a tree's lifetime.

firestorms — large fires whose need for oxygen creates its own winds.

fire years — years when severe drought combined with other factors such as high winds contributes to a large number of wildfires.

fuel — in regard to wildfire, all the dead and living material that will burn. This includes dead branches and pine needles on the ground as well as standing live and dead trees.

Greater Yellowstone Area — the public and private lands which include Yellowstone Park and surrounding national forests.

ladder — plants growing in the understory of a forest which allow fires to climb up into the canopy.

let burn — a commonly-used term to indicate a policy of allowing naturally ignited fires to burn under specific management prescriptions without initial fire suppression.

litter — the dead debris including pine cones, pine needles, branches and other material which covers the ground under a forest or shrub area.

old growth timber — a forest consisting of uneven-aged, multi-layered structures, which includes very large, old trees along with younger, shorter trees.

pathogens — disease-causing agents.

prescribed burns — fires purposely set under specific conditions.

sedimentation — dirt, gravel or sand deposited by erosion in streams or lakes.

self-prune — some tree species like lodgepole pine lose their lower branches as they grow creating a branch-free trunk which may extend most of the way to the crown of the tree.

serotinous cones — cones which have a waxy seal which keeps cone scales from opening until heated.

Sheepeaters — small group of Shoshone Indians who subsisted on bighorn sheep among other animals. They were the only year-round Indian residents of Yellowstone.

snags — dead trees.

sub-alpine forest — moist forested areas located below the limits of timber growth known as timberline.

suckers — stems which sprout from the roots of an existing plant. Aspen typically sprouts suckers.

temperature inversions — where a layer of warm air traps a denser colder layer beneath it. Typically, the higher one goes in elevation the colder the air, but in an inversion this is reversed—hence the name inversion.

thermal convection currents — air currents set up by daytime heating and nighttime cooling of air masses.

understory — plants growing in the lower levels of a forest; usually shade-tolerant species.

ungulates — hooved big-game species like deer, elk, and moose.

wind throw — trees toppled by high winds.

winter range — the low elevation areas which are usually snow-free in most winters where big game animals like elk can find uncovered forage (food).

Yellowstone Plateau — the central region of Yellowstone Park; a relatively flat ancient volcanic caldera surrounded by high mountains.

CHRONOLOGY OF IMPORTANT EVENTS OF THE 1988 GREATER YELLOWSTONE FIRE SEASON

May 24th. Rose Fire— First fire of summer. Lightning strikes tree in Lamar Valley to start the 1988 fire season. Fire went out within hours due to heavy rains.

June 14th. Storm Creek Fire— Lightning strike on lower Storm Creek on Montana's Custer National Forest begins fire. Later on in the summer, the Storm Creek Fire would threaten Cooke City and Silver Gate outside of the northeast entrance to the park forcing evacuation of the town.

June 23th. Shoshone Fire— Lightning strike near Shoshone Lake in the southern part of the park starts fire in dead, beetle-killed lodgepole pine. This fire smoldered slowly for several weeks, but later grew large enough to threaten Grant Village, forcing evacuation.

June 25th. Fan Creek Fire— Lightning strike in the Gallatin Range in the northwest part of the park starts Fan Creek fire.

June 30th. Fan Fire has grown to 35 acres.

July 1st. Fan Fire is swelled by high winds to 145 acres. The same lightning storm which produced the high winds that enlarged Fan Fire starts Red Fire in the southern portion of the park approximately four miles from Shoshone Fire.

July 8th. Fan Fire has grown to 1,800 acres. Red and Shoshone Fires still under 100 acres.

July 9th. Lightning strike starts Mist Fire near upper Lamar River drainage near eastern border of park.

July 10th. Light rain cools flames, but is last rain for two months.

July 11th. Mink Creek Fire—ignited by lighting in the Teton Wilderness on the Bridger Teton National Forest south of the park. Clover Fire is started on eastern boundary of park by lightning produced by the same storm.

July 12th. Falls Fire in southwest part of park is ignited by lightning.

July 14th. Fan Fire now 2,900 acres. Mink Creek Fire blew up from 1,000 acres to 3,000 acres in less than 24 hours. Clover Fire up to 4,700.

July 15th. Bridger-Teton Fire Management Plan calls for suppression of any fires which exceed 1,000 acres. Mink Creek Fire is attacked by 500 firefighters. Yellowstone National Park decides to begin suppression of all new fires, regardless of cause. Total acreage burned thus far—8,600 acres.

July 16th. Mink Fire up to 4,000 acres. Clover Fire is now 6,500-7,000 acres. Shoshone Fire is still relatively small at 72 acres.

July 17th. Fire crews sent to battle Falls Fire, now 140 acres in size. Mink Creek Fire doubles overnight and is 9,200 acres.

July 18th. Mink Creek Fire burns north into Yellowstone and is now 13,500 acres.

July 22th. Firewood cutter on Targhee National Forest tosses away a cigarette and starts North Fork Fire. Firefighters with bulldozers immediately detailed to blaze. Erratic winds hinder containment efforts. Same winds fan the Shoshone fire from 160 acres to more than 1000 acres.

July 23th. Strong winds blow North Fork Fire to 500 acres. Shoshone Fire doubles to 2,000 acres. Grant Village is evacuated. Clover Fire moves southward at rapid rate and merges with Mist Fire and the combined fires have now charred 31,500 acres. Storm Creek Fire gains new strength and races southward till stopped by a backfire, where it dies to a smolder.

July 24th. Shoshone Fire rapidly advancing towards Grant Village and has grown to 4,500 acres. 500 firefighters battling this one blaze. North Fork Fire still less than 1000 acres. Fire crews pulled off this blaze as they are needed to fight fires elsewhere in the park. Mink Creek Fire is now 22,500 acres and crosses into the park from adjacent Forest Service land.

July 25th. Shoshone Fire, now 9,000 acres, crosses highway and firelines to threaten Grant Village.

July 27th. Clover-Mist Fire now over 46,800 acres in size. Shoshone Fire is 10,000 acres. To date, 88,615 acres have burned. Nevertheless, Secretary of Interior, Donald Hodel, after arriving in Yellowstone to review the fire situation, reaffirms the long term beneficial influence of fire in the Yellowstone ecosystem.

July 28th. Clover-Mist grew overnight by more than twenty thousand acres to 68,035 acres. North flank of Shoshone Fire contained.

August 1st. Fan Fire, slowly growing, and now more than 10,000 acres, threatens to burn north out of park onto private land owned by Church Universal and Triumphant. Church leaders threaten to sue Park Service for any damages. Fire crew working to contain.

August 2nd. Shoshone Fire flares up and burns 6,000 acres to grow to 19,100, but Grant Village no longer threatened. Fan Fire now 16,000 acres, and bulldozers are located near northern boundary of park for suppression effort.

August 10th. Fan Fire, now 20,260 acres, has 1,529 firefighters on it. To date, 44 fires have burned 195,157 acres in park.

August 12th. Fan Fire dies down. Crews mopping up. North Fork Fire has grown to 52,960 acres and has burned to within sight of Madison-Old Faithful Road.

August 15th. Hellroaring Fire is started north of the park on the Gallatin National Forest when a spark from a horseshoe starts brush on fire.

August 20th. "Black Saturday." Fires blew up as winds of 80 mph fanned flames throughout the Park and doubled the size of fires overnight. Clover-Mist fire raced towards Cooke City while North Fork Fire swept through the Norris Geyser Basin like a runaway train. The Storm Creek Fire, nearly dead, sprang to life and, pushed by winds, ran ten miles in three hours!

August 21. The human-caused Huck Fire begins burning south of the park in Bridger-Teton National Forest.

August 23th. Clover-Mist Fire's advance towards Cooke City stopped by firefighters.

August 24th. North Fork Fire moving towards Canyon Village. Tourists and workers are evacuated from development. Huck Fire has grown to 6,000 acres.

August 25th. North Fork blaze is 108,000 acres and the eastern portion which threatened Canyon Village is renamed the Wolf Lake Fire.

August 27th. Bulldozers cut 120 foot wide firelines along park's western boundary in an effort to contain North Fork Fire.

August 31st. Red-Shoshone Fires join Mink Fire.

Sept. 1st. Western portion of North Fork Fire makes run towards the town of West Yellowstone and comes within 2 miles. Over 9,000 firefighters are now battling park blazes.

Sept. 2nd. A backfire set by West Yellowstone diverts North Fork Fire away from town. High winds drive North Fork Fire across 120 foot wide bulldozer lines, through clearcuts and threatens Moose Creek summer home development. Fan Fire is declared contained.

Sept. 4th. Storm Creek Fire threatens Cooke City and Silver Gate forcing residents to evacuate.

Sept. 7th. Backfire set to protect Cooke City is shifted by wind and burns within fifty feet of town. North Fork Fire bears down on Old Faithful Inn and firestorm nearly engulfs the historic structure. A shift in wind deflects the fire around the development.

Sept. 9th. Huck Fire has merged with Mink Fire. North Fork Fire threatens Mammoth. Facilities closed.

Sept. 10th. Winds increase and fires lunge towards park headquarters at Mammoth. Entire park is closed for the first time all summer. Mammoth evacuated.

Sept. 11th. Snow! First measurable precipitation of significance in two months slows all fires. Cool temperatures and precipitation allows firefighters to suppress or contain most fires. Park reopens. This was the turning point of the fire season. From this date there was no further threat from fires. The 1988 fire season was over except for mop up operations.

Just as a river changes throughout the season, a landscape changes over time. Fires are one of the chief agents of transformation in Yellowstone Park. Soda Butte Creek. Photo by George Wuerthner.

BIBLIOGRAPHY

Throughout this book I refer continuously to "scientists," and the work they have done on fire ecology I term "research" and "studies." For those who wish to learn more about fire behavior or ecology, the following partial list of my references may be useful.

Anderson, Stanley. *Wildlife Habitat Changes Following 1976 Wildfires on the Seney National Wildlife Refuge*. U.S. Fish and Wildlife Department publication.

Arno, Stephen. "Forest Fire History in the Northern Rockies," *Journal of Forestry*, Vol. 78, No. 8, Aug. 1980.

Arno, Stephen, and K.M. Sneck. *A Method for Determining Fire History in Coniferous Forests in the Mountain West*. U.S. Forest Service Gen. Tech. Report INT-42.

Brown, James K. *Fire Effects and Application of Prescribed Fire in Aspen*. Rangeland Fire Effects Symposium. Boise, Idaho 1984.

Cole, Walter, and Gene D. Amman. *Mountain Pine Beetle Dynamics in Lodgepole Pine Forests: Course of an Infestation*. U.S. Forest Service. Tech. Report INT-89.

DeByle, Norbert. "Managing Wildlife Habitat with Fire in the Aspen Ecosystem." In *Proceedings: Fire's Effects on Wildlife Habitat*. Gen. Tech. Report INT-186.

DeByle, Norbert, and Robert Winokur. *Aspen: Ecology and Management in the Western United States*. U.S. Forest Service Gen. Tech. Report RM-119.

Despain, Don. "Nonpyrogenous Climax Lodgepole Pine Communities in Yellowstone National Park." *Ecology*, 64(2) 1983: 231-234.

Despain, Don, and Robert Sellers. "Natural Fire in Yellowstone National Park." *Western Wildlands*, Summer 1977.

Fischer, William and Bruce D. Clayton. *Fire Ecology of Montana Forest Types East of the Continental Divide*. Gen. Tech. Report INT-141.

Gruell, George. *Fire's Influence on Wildlife Habitat on the Bridger-Teton National Forest, Wyoming*. U.S. Forest Service Research Paper INT-252.

_____. "The Importance of Fire in the Greater Yellowstone Ecosystem." *Western Wildlands*, Fall 1986.

Gruell, George, et. al. *Seventy Years of Vegetative Change in a Managed Ponderosa Pine Forest in Western Montana*. U.S. Forest Service Gen Tech. Report INT-130.

Habeck, James. *Fire Ecology Investigations in Selway-Bitterroot Wilderness*. U.S. Forest Service Publication R1-72-001.

Habeck, James, and Robert Mutch. "Fire-dependent Forests in the Northern Rocky Mountains." *Quaternary Research*, 3: 408-424.

Houston, Douglas. *The Northern Yellowstone Elk: Ecology and Management*. New York: Macmillan.

_____. "Wildfires in Northern Yellowstone Park." *Ecology*, 54:1111-1117.

Kirsch, Leo, and Arnold Kruse. "Praire Fires and Wildlife:" In *Proceedings: Tall Timbers Fire Ecology Conference*. 1972.

Koch, Elder. *When the Mountains Roared: Stories of the 1910 Fire*. Idaho Panhandle National Forests Publication.

Komarek, Edwin V. "Fire: Control, Ecology, and Management." In *Proceedings in Fire Management in the Northern Environment*. 1979.

Lotan, James E. and David Perry. *Ecology and Regeneration of Lodgepole Pine*. Agriculture Handbook 606.

Lotan, James E. et. al. *Effects of Fire on Flora*. U.S. Forest Service Gen. Tech. Report WO-16

Lyon, Jack, et. al. *Effects of Fire on Fauna*. U.S. Forest Service Gen. Tech. Report WO-6.

Manns, Timothy. Unpublished historical account of Yellowstone Park fires.

McClelland, Riley. "Wildlife Influences on Aesthetic Values in Glacier National Park." *Western Wildlands*, Summer 1977.

Mutch, Robert. "Fire Management and Land Use Planning Today." *Western Wildlands*, Winter, 1976.

Park Service Staff. *Wildland Fire Management Plan for Yellowstone National Park*. 1987.

Proceedings: Symposium and Workshops on Wilderness Fire. Includes the following papers:

Arno, Stephen. "Ecological Effects and Management Implications of Indian Fires."

Brown, James K. "The Unnatural Fuel Build-up Issue:"

Condon, Michael K. "Economic Analysis for Wilderness Fire Management: A Care Study."

Despain, Don. "Ecological Implications of Ignition Sources in Park and Wilderness Fire Management Programs."

Gruell, George. "Indian Fires in Interior West: A Widespread Influence."

Habeck, James. "Impact of Fire Suppression on Forest Succession and Fuel Accumulations in Long-Fire-Interval Wilderness Habitat Types."

Heinselman, Miron. "Fire Regimes and Management in Ecosystems with Large High-Intensity Fires."

Keown, Larry. "Fire Behavior Prediction Techniques For Park and Wilderness Fire Planning."

Mills, Thomas J. "Criteria for Evaluating the Economic Efficiency of Fire Management Programs in Park and Wilderness Areas." Gen. Tech. Report INT-182.

Pyne, Stephen J. *Fire in America*. Princeton University Press, 1982.

Romme, William H. *Fire and Landscape Diversity in Subalpine Forests of Yellowstone National Park*. Ecological Monographs 52(2) 1982, 199-221.

Romme, William H. and Dennis H. Knight. "Landscape Diversity: The Concept Applied to Yellowstone Park." *BioScience*, Vol. 32, No.8.

Schroeder, Mark, and Charles Buck. *Fire Weather*. Agriculture Handbook 360.

Taylor, Dale. "Biotic Succession of Lodgepole Pine Forests of Fire Origin in Yellowstone National Park." *National Geographic Society Research Reports*, Vol. 12: 693-702.

_____. "Forest Fires and the Tree-Hole Nesting Cycle in Grand Teton and Yellowstone National Parks." In *Proceedings: First Conference on Scientific Research in the National Parks*, Vol. 1, 1976.

_____. "Forest Fires in Yellowstone National Park." *Journal of Forest History*, July 1974. 69-77.

Tiedemann, Arthur R. et. al. *Effects of Fire on Water*. U.S. Forest Service Gen. Tech. Report WO-10.

Vogl, Richard. "Ecologically Sound Management: Modern Man's Road to Survival." *Western Wildlands*, Summer 1977.

Wells, Carol G. et. al. *Effects of Fire on Soil*. U.S. Forest Service Gen. Tech. Report WO-7.

AUTHOR'S NOTE

George Wuerthner is a freelance writer and photographer who lives in Livingston, Montana, just north of Yellowstone National Park. He is the author of five books covering natural history topics including *Alaska Mountain Ranges, Oregon Mountain Ranges, Idaho Mountain Ranges, Forever Wild—The Adirondack Mountains* and *Vermont—A Portrait of the Land and Its People*. His photographs have appeared in many national publications and calendars. Prior to becoming a full-time freelance writer, the author had been employed as a botanist, range technician, forestry technician, wilderness ranger, high school teacher and university instructor. He has undergraduate degrees in both wildlife biology and botany and a master's degree in science communication.